TIGER CUBS

JEN BESEL

BLACK RABBIT BOOKS

Bolt Jr. is published by Black Rabbit Books
P.O. Box 3263, Mankato, Minnesota, 56002.
www.blackrabbitbooks.com

Michael Sellner, designer; Omay Ayres, photo researcher

Names: Besel, Jennifer M., author.
Title: Tiger cubs / by Jen Besel.
Description: Mankato, Minnesota : Black Rabbit Books, [2020] | Series: Bolt Jr. baby animals | Includes bibliographical references and index. | Audience: Age 6-8. | Audience: K to Grade 3.
Identifiers: LCCN 2019001753 (print) | LCCN 2019002721 (ebook) | ISBN 9781623101497 (ebook) | ISBN 9781623101435 (library binding) | ISBN 9781644660997 (paperback)
Subjects: LCSH: Tiger cubs—Juvenile literature.
Classification: LCC QL737.C23 (ebook) | LCC QL737.C23 B474 2020 (print) | DDC 599.75613/92—dc23
LC record available at https://lccn.loc.gov/2019001753

Printed in the United States. 5/19

Image Credits

Alamy: Eugen Wais, 10–11; Joe Vogan, 16–17; Mark Malkinson, 6–7; Nature Picture Library, 12, 18–19; Getty: AFP, 5; Shutterstock: Africa Studio, 23; Anan Kaewkhammul, 4, 8–9, 10, 13; apiguide, 1; EhayDy, Cover; Eric Isselee, 21 (inset); Natalliya85, 3, 24; okili77, 14 (tiger); Olga Kovalenko, 7 (apples); Yotin Pilaisomboon, 20–21

Contents

CHAPTER 1

Playful Babies

A mother tiger sits in the grass. Cubs play nearby. They run around. They **pounce** on each other. They even **pretend** to bite. Soon they will have to hunt for supper. But for now they can play.

pounce: to suddenly jump toward something

pretend: to make believe

WEIGHT COMPARISON

newborn cub
2 to 3 pounds
(1 to 1.4 kilograms)

Growing Fast

Tigers are powerful hunters. But they don't start that way. Newborn cubs are blind and toothless. They need their mothers to keep them safe. But cubs grow fast. They soon get teeth. They learn to walk and play.

9 apples
about 3 pounds (1.4 kg)

PARTS OF A

Tiger Cub

ears
whiskers

CHAPTER 2

Food and Homes

Cubs **chase** and play a lot. They get hungry. At first, cubs drink their mothers' milk. But after just a few weeks, they start eating meat. Mothers bring cubs deer and pig meat.

chase: to follow quickly in order to catch

FACT

Mothers call to cubs with a roar.

Home Sweet Home

Cubs are born in dens. These are warm, safe homes. Once cubs get bigger, they leave the dens. They explore their world. Tigers live in forests, **swamps**, or grasslands.

swamp: land that is always wet and often covered in water

Tiger Range

Asia

CHAPTER 3

Growing Up

Cubs must learn to hunt. Mothers won't bring them food forever. Cubs watch their mothers. Then they copy their actions.

FACT

By 18 months old, cubs hunt on their own.

Their Own Homes

Cubs live with their mothers until they're about two years old. Then they look for homes of their own.

The young tigers keep growing for a while. By five years old, they'll have cubs of their own.

660

Adult Tiger's Weight

up to 660 pounds
(299 kg)

Bonus Facts

Cubs lose their **baby teeth.**

Tigers like to swim.

No two tigers have the same stripes.

Tigers live **10 to 15 years** in the **wild**.

wild: not living in a house or zoo

READ MORE/WEBSITES

Brown, Margaret Wise. *Be Brave, Little Tiger!* Bath, UK: Parragon, 2018.

Kelley, K.C. *Baby Tigers.* Baby Animals. Mankato, MN: Amicus, 2018.

Nilsen, Genevieve. *Tiger Cubs.* Safari Babies. Minneapolis: Jump!, Inc., 2019.

Tiger
kids.nationalgeographic.com/animals/tiger/#ww-wild-cats-tiger.jpg

Tiger
kids.sandiegozoo.org/animals/tiger

Tiger
www.ducksters.com/animals/tiger.php

GLOSSARY

chase (CHAYS)—to follow quickly in order to catch

pounce (POWNS)—to suddenly jump toward something

pretend (pree-TEND)—to make believe

swamp (SWAMP)—land that is always wet and often covered in water

wild (WIHLD)—not living in a house or zoo

INDEX